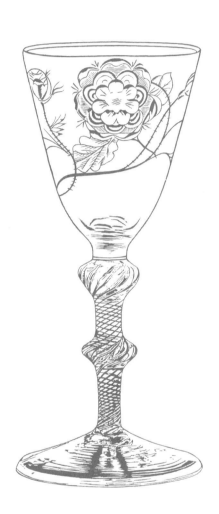

THE DRAMBUIE COLLECTION

The Art Collection of
The Drambuie Liqueur Company

First published 1995 by
The Drambuie Liqueur Company
Edinburgh
Copyright © 1995 The Drambuie Liqueur Company

ISBN 0 9525548 0 1

Text: Robin Nicholson
Catalogue: Robin Nicholson & George Neilson
Production and Publishing Consultant: Paul Harris
Photography: Jack Mackenzie
Printed in Slovenia by Gorenjski Tisk

CONTENTS

Plate 1

William Simson (1800-1847)
Prince Charlie at Holyrood

oil on panel 9 x 7 inches signed and dated 1833 (bottom left)

This sketch for a painting exhibited at the Royal Scottish Academy in 1834 shows Prince Charles Edward Stuart reading the despatch from General Cope which placed a bounty of £30,000 on his head. Simson, who was a pupil of Wilkie, was, like many artists of his generation, greatly impressed by Walter Scott's romantic re-interpretation of the Jacobite story.

Foreword

Drambuie has always been proud of its Scottish heritage. The origins of this uniquely Scottish drink lie with the MacKinnon Clan of Skye, who helped the desperate Prince Charles Edward Stuart when on the run after Culloden. With no possessions remaining, the Prince gave a secret recipe to one of the Clan as reward for their invaluable assistance. This recipe was for a personal liqueur, a mixture of herbs, honey and whisky, and this liqueur is what we now know as 'Drambuie' - *the drink that satisfies*. It is still made by descendants of the MacKinnons of Skye and the recipe remains a secret to this day.

The art collection of The Drambuie Liqueur Company is intended to reflect the rich artistic culture and history of Scotland and, by so doing, be a reflection of the qualities of Drambuie itself. The collection has two main themes. The first is the wonderful and diverse works of art that were produced by the supporters of Prince Charles Edward Stuart - the 'Jacobites' - during the 18th century. Paintings, prints, miniatures medals and, above all, drinking glasses, for the Jacobites loved nothing better than to raise a toast to their exiled King. Our collection of Jacobite glass is agreed to be the finest in existence.

The second strand to the collection is paintings by Scottish artists, mostly of the 19th and early 20th centuries. It is a fine, relatively small, collection, that nonetheless contains some superb paintings by some of the best known artists of the period. It is a source of unending pleasure to be able to look at such fine works of art within a working environment.

The art collection has been comparatively little known until now. But it is hoped that over the years it will be seen, not only by visitors to the company, but by a broader public, through publications such as this one and through exhibitions. It is gratifying to think that Drambuie can return something to the culture and heritage of the country which has given it so much.

It is 250 years since Charles Edward Stuart - 'Bonnie Prince Charlie' - set foot on Scottish soil and the history of Drambuie began. It is a fitting year for the publication of this book which contains a selection of some of the finest works of art in the Drambuie Collection.

Malcolm MacKinnon   Duncan MacKinnon

The Drambuie Liqueur Company
1995

The Drambuie Collection
of
Jacobite Works of Art

Plate 2

*Hand-painted fan with portrait of Prince
Charles Edward Stuart and allegorical
representations of Scotland, England
and Ireland*

- Jacobite Works of Art -

On the 22nd of July 1745, Prince Charles Edward Stuart set foot on the Isle of Eriskay in the Outer Hebrides. This signalled the beginning of the most ambitious attempt by the Stuart Royal Family to regain the thrones of Great Britain and Ireland, lost in the so-called 'Glorious Revolution' of 1689. The Rising of 1745 was to enter history as a monument to hope, courage and fidelity and its resonances, romanticised and, sometimes, simplified, can still be heard today.

The Royal House of Stuart, a dynasty descended from Robert the Bruce, had ruled Scotland for three hundred years until 1603 when King James VI of Scotland inherited the English throne and became King of both countries. Less than a hundred years later his grandson, King James VII & II was forced to flee to France after anti-Catholic factions in parliament invited the Protestant William of Orange to invade Britain and take the throne. He never returned to his Kingdom and died in exile in 1701. Parliament immediately passed an act to prevent his heirs inheriting and ensure a Protestant succession. Their machinations reached final fruition when, in 1715, George, Elector of Hanover, a man with no legitimate claim, was asked to become King. A Stuart was never to reign in Britain again.

The Cause of James's son, who became known as James VIII & III (or the 'Old Pretender' to those who did not recognise him) and his son, Prince Charles Edward Stuart (the'Young Pretender') was undoubtedly a just one and they had many followers both in exile and in Britain, who were appalled at the denial of legitimacy and the disregard for the Divine Right of Kings. These supporters became known as 'Jacobites', after the Latin for 'James', and the period from 1689 until Charles's death in 1788 saw repeated attempts by the Jacobites to re-instate their lawful and rightful monarchy. The Rising of 1745 came closest to success as an army of Highlanders, led by their 'Bonnie Prince Charlie', almost succeeded in returning the Crown of Great Britain to the ancient Royal Family of Scotland.

The Jacobite Cause was, by and large, concerned with loyalty and it was a matter of concern, both to the exiled Stuarts and to their followers, that this loyalty should be expressed. This was done in the written word, in poetry, in the observation and commemoration of certain dates but, above all, it was done by the commissioning, the cherishing and the possession of works of art. It was considered essential that the follower of the Cause should be constantly reminded of the nature and appearance of the Stuart king and the justness of his claim. Works of art, particularly those bearing a likeness of the exiled sovereign, were deemed to act as a surrogate for the affections and loyalty of the subject.

It was inevitable, therefore, that the exiled Jacobite Court - first based at St. Germain, near Paris and, from 1720, in Rome - took a great interest in the production and distribution of works of art. This inclination is most apparent in the use of medals, (*Plates 37, 38*) which were commissioned to celebrate almost any occasion and immediately sent over to Britain in large quantities. Some of these, engraved by the finest craftsmen of Paris and Rome, are exquisite examples of the medallist's skills and are the continuation of a great European medallic tradition which had its origins in the Renaissance.

Inevitably, paintings, and the engravings copied from them, were the most accessible way in which the image and attributes of the King could be transmitted to his followers. It was believed that his features were imbued with the divine radiance of monarchy and by looking upon them the viewer would be reminded of his legitimacy. A motto that often appears is 'Look, Love and Follow', suggesting that loyalty will be the inevitable consequence of gazing upon the royal countenance.

The Jacobite Royal Family engaged many of the leading European artists of the age to paint their portraits, notably, in France, François de Troy (*Plates 4, 5*) and, in Rome, Antonio David (*Plate 25*). These portraits were copied and engraved in large numbers, sometimes by studio followers of the artist, sometimes by speculative copyists with an eye to a ready market. The style of the portraits is derived from the tradition of Court painting that flourished under the Stuarts in England in the 17th century, where the trappings of kingship and the qualities of martial valour are always at the forefront. Even in the most intimate portraits, James and his sons Charles and Henry, always wear the blue sash of the Order of the Garter, an ancient Order of Knighthood, long the personal gift of the legitimate sovereign.

Prince Charles Edward Stuart was painted throughout his childhood and the engravings taken from these pictures provided his supporters in Britain with a running commentary on his development. By the time of the '45 his reputation as a charismatic and vigorous warrior was well established. The decision to launch the Rising in Scotland resulted in Charles assuming a distinctly Highland Scottish *persona*, something he went to pains to encourage by wearing tartan and a Highland bonnet (although never a kilt). Artists in Britain and abroad swiftly accommodated this development and adapted existing portraits, adding tartan and other Scottish accoutrements (*Plates 28, 30*). Charles was well-suited to the role of Highland Prince and was often equated with another exiled Prince - the classical hero, Aeneas (*Plates 31, 20*).

The amount of copying of portraits of Charles that occurred inevitably resulted in many crude images, where the physical likeness is absent and only the presence of tartan identifies the sitter. However, the bust, sculpted in Paris three years after the '45 by Lemoyne (*Plate 27*) was considered an extremely good likeness and readily captures the assertive carriage of the head and self-confident demeanour that characterised the young Stuart heir.

The failure of the 1745 Rising and the gradual lessening of Jacobite hopes in the years afterwards saw a decrease in the production of specifically propagandist works of art; the commissioning of medals, for example, was dramatically reduced. At the same time, however, there remained a strong feeling of sentimental Jacobitism amongst supporters in Britain, an idealistic and romantic admiration for the Stuarts which, while intense, would never again be matched with active physical support. These twilight years of Jacobite aspirations saw the appearance of works of art that were expressive of both the loyalty and the sense of loss and are, perhaps, the most beautiful and enduring artistic legacy of the Jacobite era - engraved glass.

Glass-making was a well established industry in Britain. The invention of lead crystal by George Ravenscroft in the 1670s meant that English glass was the finest and clearest available and constant innovation in the making and engraving of glass took place throughout the 18th century. By the middle of the century, drinking glasses, glass bowls and decanters were in widespread use amongst all but the poor and were certainly always to be found on the table at times of conviviality.

Sentimental Jacobitism thrived on conviviality and many of the serious Jacobite groups of the 1720s and 30s had become little more than drinking clubs by the 1750s. The use of glasses, engraved with explicit or implicit symbols, was rapidly adopted by the established clubs and by smaller informal groups. Although documentation is scarce, it has been established that well over one hundred Jacobite clubs existed in England and Wales in the 1750s and 60s. In Scotland, where destruction of the Highland way of life was well under way, there are fewer known clubs or societies. One that is well documented, however, and is probably typical, is the club that met annually to commemorate the birthday of Prince Charles (31st December) in St. James Square in Edinburgh and drank toasts from glasses enamelled with a portrait of Charles (*Plate 3*). Their last meeting, attended by the poet Robert Burns, was a month before Charles's death.

The one type of glass that is thought to predate the '45 are the 'Amen' glasses. There are about thirty-five of these known, the example in the Drambuie Collection (*Plate 6*) being one of the largest and finest. Engraved entirely free-hand with a diamond point, the glasses usually bear some or all of the verses of the Jacobite anthem (now adapted to the British National Anthem) surrounding a cypher for 'James VIII' and the prominent word 'Amen', translating in this instance as 'Let it be' (i.e. the Stuart restoration). The reference to James VIII of Scotland suggests the glasses were engraved north of the border and the assertive celebratory use of the anthem might indicate the glasses had a more polemic than sentimental motive.

The post-1745 glasses are all engraved by copper wheel, a skilled process involving the use of a foot treadle and bench tool. The identity of the engravers is, of course, unknown. However, through the later glasses their runs a distinctive iconography, a re-use and adaptation of images, symbols and mottoes, suggesting there was a certain degree of affinity between the craftsmen, or at least a knowledge of each others work. Some images are almost ubiquitous: the rose and two buds representing James and his two heirs; the oak leaf and the thistle; the moth, symbolising the 'return of the soul'. Likewise some of the mottoes re-appear frequently: 'Fiat' (*Let it be*), 'Redeat' (*May he return*), 'Revirescit' (*Let it grow again*); others are less common, or more allusive: 'Audentior Ibo' (*Go more boldly*) , 'Turno Tempus Erit' (*For Turnus there will be a time*). Portraits of Prince Charles are rare and the Drambuie Collection has one of the finest groups (*Plates 7, 8, 9, 10, 15, 18e, 23*)

The glasses themselves were probably made in any one of the main glass-making towns in Britain - Edinburgh, Glasgow, Newcastle, London - and are as varied in their construction as they are in their engraving. Some have bubbles of air or enamel twisted into the stems; some are elongated to make high bowled glasses for champagne or ratafia; others flattened and attached to heavy bases, intended to be slammed sharply on the table with a firing noise after a toast. Larger cups and glasses would have been passed around a table for communal drinking; finger bowls would be placed so that the drinker could pass his glass 'over the water' during the toast to the 'King', making it clear where his true sovereign was to be found.

It is not clear how grave an offence it was to possess a Jacobite glass (or, indeed, any similar work of art) in the post-1745 period, but certainly a degree of concealment and circumspection was required. For this reason and because of their vulnerability it is likely that many of the glasses have not survived the passage of time. The Drambuie Collection is remarkable, therefore, not just in the range and diversity of Jacobite glasses in its collection, but in their exemplary state of preservation.

With the death of Charles Edward Stuart in 1788, the hopes of a Stuart restoration ended forever. The Jacobites may have lost their cause, but they left a rich legacy of works of art that embody both their loyalties and their appreciation of fine craftsmanship and artistry. It is intended that the Drambuie Collection of Jacobite Works of Art should reflect these virtues.

Further Reading:

Rosalind Marshall (ed.) *Dynasty: the Royal House of Stewart* National Galleries of Scotland 1990

Geoffrey Seddon, *The Jacobites and their Drinking Glasses* Antique Collectors Club 1995

Plate 3

*Wine Glass with enamel portrait of
Prince Charles Edward Stuart c.1775*

Plate 4
François de Troy (1645-1730)
James VIII & III, c. 1704

Plate 5
circle of François de Troy (1645-1730)
Princess Louisa Maria Stuart

Plate 6

The 'Spottiswoode' Amen Glass c. 1745

Plate 7

Wine Glass c. 1750

Plate 8

Tumbler c. 1750

Plate 9

Large Goblet c. 1750

Plate 10

Spirit Tumbler c. 1750

Plate 11

Wine Glass c. 1750

Plate 12

Shaft and Globe Decanter c. 1750

Plate 13

Wine Glass c. 1760

Plate 14

Loving Cup c. 1750

Plate 15

Wine Glass c. 1750

Plate 16

Large Covered Goblet c. 1750

Plate 17

Wine Flask c. 1746

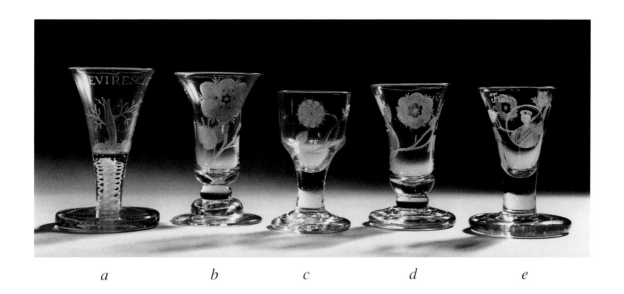

a   b   c   d   e

a   b   c   d   e

Plate 18

a) Firing Glass c. 1765 b) Jelly or Syllabub Glass c. 1750
c) Toasting Glass c. 1750 d) Toasting Glass c. 1750 e) Firing Glass c. 1760

Plate 19

a) Waterglass c. 1750 b) Spirit Tumbler c. 1780 c) Glass Rinser c. 1780
d) Glass Mug c. 1780 e) Tumbler c. 1745

29

Plate 20

Wine Glass c. 1750

a   b   c   d   e

a   b   c   d

Plate 21

a) Pair of Cordial Glasses c. 1745 b) Ratafia Wine Glass c. 1760
c) Champagne Flute c. 1750 d) Cordial Glass c. 1745 e) Wine Glass c. 1745

Plate 22

a) Wine Glass c. 1745 b) Wine Glass c. 1745
c) Cordial Glass c. 1745 d) Wine Glass c. 1750

31

Plate 23

Wine Glass c. 1750

Plate 24

after Antonio David (1702-1766)
Miniature of Prince Charles Edward Stuart

Plate 25

Antonio David (1702-1766)
Prince Charles Edward Stuart Prince Henry Benedict Stuart c. 1734

Plate 26

Cosmo Alexander (1724-1772)
Prince Charles Edward Stuart, 1752

Plate 27

Jean-Baptiste Lemoyne (1704-1778)
Bust of Prince Charles Edward Stuart, 1746

Plate 28

after Sir Robert Strange (1721-1792)
Prince Charles Edward Stuart in Tartan

Plate 29

James Ferguson (1710-1776)
Prince Charles Edward Stuart

Plate 30

Continental School, mid-18th Century
Portrait of Prince Charles Edward Stuart

Plate 31

Sir Robert Strange (1721-1792)
Prince Charles Edward Stuart, 1745

Plate 32

after Louis Tocque (1696-1772)
Prince Charles Edward Stuart, 1748

Mrs. Flora Macdonald

Mrs. Flora Macdonald

Plate 33

after Allan Ramsay (1713-1784)
Flora MacDonald

Plate 34

after Thomas Hudson (1701-1779)
Flora MacDonald

Plate 35

after Thomas Hudson (1701-1779)
Benn's Club of Aldermen

Plate 36

attributed to Cosmo Alexander (1724-1772)
A Jacobite Lady, possibly Jenny Cameron of Glendessary

a   b   c

d

Plate 37

A Selection of Medals 1689-1720

42

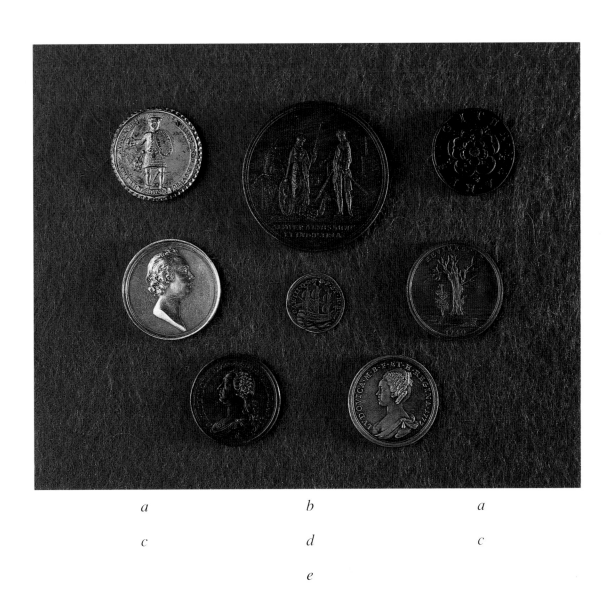

a   *b*   *a*

c   *d*   *c*

e

Plate 38

A Selection of Medals 1749-1772

- Jacobite Works of Art -

Plate 2

A JACOBITE FAN, c.1746 parchment leaf painted with gouache and ink, carved ivory sticks Radius: 11 inches

This extremely rare fan, which may have been made in France, shows a portrait of Prince Charles being offered tribute by three allegorical figures representing Ireland, England and Scotland. The ivory guard sticks are carved with a crown, a rose, a harp, acorns, a thistle, crossed swords and the symbolic eye of God. The verso depicts St. James's Palace and a dove carrying a banner with the word 'My House shall be called the House of Prayer' (possibly equating Charles's mission with that of Christ's when he drove the money-lenders from the Temple).

Plate 3

ENAMEL PORTRAIT WINE GLASS, opaque twist stem of two five ply spirals, c.1775 Height: 5¼ inches

An extremely rare Jacobite wine glass from an original group of only six which combine these colours. The portrait is based on the engraving by Strange and the glasses were made for Thomas Erskine, later 9th Earl of Kellie. They were used by a group of Jacobite sympathisers who met annually, in Edinburgh, on the anniversary of Prince Charles's birth. A guest at their final dinner in 1787 was the poet Robert Burns.

Plates 4 & 5

FRANÇOIS DE TROY (1645-1730) *James VIII & III c.1704* oil on canvas 28 x 22 inches *Princess Louisa Maria Stuart* oil on canvas 28¼ x 23¼ inches

De Troy was one of the most popular portraitists at the Stuart Court at St. Germain near Paris. He painted James several times after he succeeded his father, James II, in 1701. The recent restoration of this painting has revealed extensive underdrawing suggesting that this may be the primary work in the series that is known to have been painted by the artist in the 1704-05 period.
The portrait of Princess Louisa, only surviving sister of James, was painted in 1701 and may be by an assistant of De Troy. It formerly belonged to the Howard family, who were staunch Jacobites in northern England.

Plate 6

THE 'SPOTTISWOODE' AMEN GLASS, air twist stem, engraved in diamond point on bowl c.1745 Height: 8¼ inches

This is one of the finest and best preserved 'Amen' glasses in existence. It is engraved in diamond point with the Jacobite anthem, the cypher of James VIII and dedicatory inscriptions to Prince Charles and Prince Henry. The reference to James VIII (of Scotland) suggests it was engraved north of the border. The word 'Amen' - *let it be* - is prominent and gives the glasses their name. There are about thirty-five known Amen glasses, many with associations with well-known Jacobite families. John Spottiswoode of Spottiswoode in Berwickshire took up arms for Prince Charles in 1745 and this glass is thought to have descended through his family.

Plate 7

ENGRAVED PORTRAIT WINE GLASS, with rose, bud and thistle, inscribed *Audentior Ibo* ('*Go More Boldly*'), on double knop multi-spiral air-twist stem, c.1750 Height: 6 3/8 inches.

Plate 8

ENGRAVED PORTRAIT TUMBLER c.1750 Height: 4 inches

Tumblers bearing portraits are rare (a similar glass is in the Royal Scottish Museum). This example shows Prince Charles within a circular cartouche surmounted by a crown with Prince of Wales feathers and flanked by a thistle with four leaves, a six petal rose, three-quarter open and half open buds on a stem with five leaves and an oak leaf. The rim is engraved with targes, swords, bagpipes and military trophies; the base is ground away at the pontil and engraved with a sunflower. The inscription *Fiat* means '*Let it be*'.

Plate 9

LARGE ENGRAVED PORTRAIT GOBLET, multi-spiral air twist stem, inscribed *Fiat* c. 1750 Height: 7¼ inches

Unusual features of this glass include the cartouche of laurel leaves, the rose and thistle growing from the same stem and the profile portrait of Charles which faces to the right, rather than the usual left.

Plate 10

ENGRAVED PORTRAIT SPIRIT TUMBLER c.1750 Height: 4¼ inches

This unique spirit tumbler combines a portrait of Prince Charles with a crown on the reverse of the glass. When the glass is raised to the lips, the crown appears to sit on the head of the Prince.

Plate 11

WINE GLASS engraved with portrait and rose and two buds, inscribed *Audentior Ibo* ('*Go More Boldly*') c.1750 Height: 6 inches

- Jacobite Works of Art -

Plate 12

SHAFT AND GLOBE DECANTER engraved with rose and two buds, two oak leaves and bud, star, and inscribed '*Fiat*' above a compass. c.1750 Height: 7¼ inches

Shaft and globe decanters with Jacobite inscriptions are very rare. This example was formerly in the Chasleton House Collection.

Plate 13

WINE GLASS engraved with rose and buds, inscribed *Success to the Society*, on opaque multi-spiral air twist stem, c.1760 Height: 6 inches

The inscription refers to one of the Jacobite societies that existed in the North of England, Scotland and North Wales, the more notable being 'The True Blue Society', 'The Society of Sea Serjeants' and 'The Oak Society'.

Plate 14

LOVING CUP engraved with rose and bud and daffodil and bud, applied strap handles, on knopped and domed foot, c.1750 Height: 8⅝ inches

Jacobite engraved loving and drinking cups are quite rare. They would have been passed around small companies and drunk from communally. The engraved daffodil alludes to the 'Prince of Wales' (Prince Charles Edward Stuart).

Plate 15

WINE GLASS engraved with portrait of 'Betty Burke' on a double knop multi-spiral air-twist stem, c.1750 Height: 6¼ inches

The figure, holding a spray of a rose and two buds, has been identified as either 'Betty Burke' - the name adopted by Prince Charles while in disguise as Flora MacDonald's maidservant on his journey from the Outer Hebrides to Skye - or as Flora MacDonald herself. The rather ungainly figure portrayed supports the first identification.

Plate 16

LARGE COVERED GOBLET engraved with rose and bud, snakehead fritillary and buds and pink and buds, on a double series air-twist stem, c.1750 Height: 12¾ inches

A goblet of this size would probably have been used for punch. The engraving on the cover cleverly echoes the engraving on the bowl.

Plate 17

WINE OR SPIRIT FLASK engraved with stylised oak leaves, rose buds and bee, inscribed *M T A* and dated *Aug.7.1746*, c.1746 Height: 9¾ inches

Possibly a marriage flask, although the heavy section of the glass may mean its use was more for travelling. The date has no obvious significance to the Jacobite Cause and is therefore more likely to commemorate the marriage between families with Jacobite sympathies.

Plate 18

a) FIRING GLASS engraved with bare tree-trunk from which a sapling grows and the motto *Revirescit* ('*It grows again*') on a double-series opaque twist stem, c.1765 Height: 4¼ inches

This glass is of soda metal which indicates it originated from the Low Countries where soda was more commonly used in glass manufacture than lead. The engraving refers to the Jacobite hopes that a sapling (Prince Charles) would grow from the old oak (James III).

b) JELLY OR SYLLABUB GLASS engraved with six petal rose, c.1750 Height: 4¼ inches

Syllabub was a mixture of milk or cream curdled and sweetened or flavoured and mixed with wine, cider or cordial. The lower portion of the bowl contained the sweetener or flavoured wine and the wide shoulders of the ogee rim offered support for the airy froth of the whipped cream.

c) TOASTING GLASS engraved with rose and bud and sunburst, c.1750 Height: 3⅞ inches

d) TOASTING OR FIRING GLASS with bell bowl engraved with six petal rose, star and motto *Fiat*, c.1750 Height: 4 inches

e) FIRING GLASS engraved with portrait of Prince Charles, six petal rose and motto *Fiat*, c.1760 Height: 4 inches

The name firing glass refers to the noise made when the glass was banged down on a table after a toast had been drunk. Only one other example with a portrait is known.

Plate 19

a) WATERGLASS with waisted bowl, engraved with seven petal rose and bud on domed circular solid foot, c.1750 Height: 4⅝ inches

Water glasses were placed on the table so that the Jacobite toast to the 'King over the Water' might be made, that is toasting 'the King', but at the same time passing the toasting glass over the water glass on the table.

b) SPIRIT TUMBLER inscribed *Health, to all, True Blues* and engraved with six petal rose on base c.1780 Height: 3½ inches

This is a very rare tumbler, bearing the motto or toast of the True Blue Society, a Jacobite Club, and is taken from their song *True Blue*.

c) GLASS RINSER OR WATER BOWL engraved with rose and bud and moth, c.1780 Height: 2⅞ inches

Rinsers or water bowls were placed on the table to rinse glasses between wines or to wash fingers between courses. They could also be used to toast the 'King over the Water' - the glass raised and passed over the top of the waterbowl - during the loyal toast.

d) GLASS MUG, engraved with rose and buds and hovering bee and moth, with applied strap handle, c.1780 Height: 4 inches

Mugs with Jacobite engraving are extremely unusual. The moth or butterfly with extended wings represents prayers for the 'return of the soul' of the Jacobite movement, the bee, the hoped for renewal of activity after rest.

e) TUMBLER of waisted shape with rose and bud and engraved with sunflower on base, c. 1745 Height: 4 inches

The sunflower was the badge of James II as Duke of York and the image of the sun often appears in Jacobite iconography, with the Stuart King often equated with the rising sun.

Plate 20

WINE GLASS engraved with rose and buds and star and inscribed *Turno Tempus Erit* around the rim, *Fiat* on the bowl and *Redeat* on the foot, c.1750 Height: 6⅛ inches

The motto *Fiat* ('*Let it be*')is not uncommon, but the inscription *Turno Tempus Erit*, especially combined with the inscription *Redeat* is very unusual. The latter means '*May he return*', the former, '*For Turnus there shall be a time*', which equates the Hanoverians with the Virgilian character Turnus who, having killed the son of an ally of Aeneas, was in turn slain by Aeneas.

Plate 21

a) A PAIR OF CORDIAL GLASSES engraved with rose and bud on drawn multi-spiral air-twist stems, c.1745 Height: 6¼ inches

Possibly separated soon after manufacture, these glasses have only recently been re-united after two hundred and fifty years apart.

b) RATAFIA WINE GLASS engraved with rose and bud and large moth on opaque gauze core surrounded by four opaque thread stem, c.1760 Height: 7¼ inches

Ratafia was a brandy infusion in which most of the soft fruits were used: blackcurrants, strawberries, raspberries, black cherries and mulberries - all picked when fully ripe. The wine was used in toasting or 'ratifying' a treaty or agreement. The bowls and stems of these glasses are tall and slender so that they could be easily 'touched' in toasting.

c) CHAMPAGNE FLUTE engraved with rose and buds and butterfly on double knopped multi-spiral air-twist stem, c.1750 Height: 8 inches

d) CORDIAL GLASS engraved with rose and buds on multi-spiral air-twist stem, on foot engraved with oak leaves and motto *Redi* ('*Return*'), c.1745 Height: 6⅛ inches

e) WINE GLASS engraved with rose and buds, oak leaf and motto *Fiat*, on drawn multi-spiral air-twist stem, foot engraved with Prince of Wales feathers on underside c.1745 Height: 6¼ inches

Plate 22

a) WINE GLASS engraved with rose and buds on 'Newcastle' light baluster stem, c.1745 Height: 6⅞ inches

b) WINE GLASS with drawn trumpet bowl engraved with rose and bud and a star, drawn stem enclosing an elongated tear, c.1745 Height: 6¼ inches

c) CORDIAL GLASS engraved with rose and buds oak leaf and thistle and inscribed *Fiat*, on drawn stem enclosing two tears, foot engraved with Prince of Wales feathers, c.1745 Height: 5¾ inches

d) WINE GLASS with funnel bowl engraved with rose and bud and crest of *lion gardant* on 'Newcastle' baluster stem, c.1750 Height: 6¼ inches

- Jacobite Works of Art -

Plate 23

WINE GLASS engraved with portrait of Prince Charles in laurel wreath flanked by rose and bud, reverse with star, on multi-spiral air-twist stem, c.1750 Height: 6¼ inches

The star on this and other glasses refers to the belief that a new star was seen on the night of Prince Charles's birth.

Plate 24

after ANTONIO DAVID (1702-1766) *Prince Charles Edward Stuart* oil on copper 4 x 3⅛ inches

This is one of the best known portraits of Charles and is probably taken from the version now in the National Portrait Gallery. The ivory frame mounted with Cairngorm stones suggests it may have belonged to a Scottish Jacobite sympathiser.

Plate 25

ANTONIO DAVID (1702-1766) *Prince Charles Edward Stuart Prince Henry Benedict Stuart* oil on ivory each 3 inches high

These miniatures were probably painted in 1734 when Charles was fourteen and Henry nine. They are identical in composition to the pair of full-size portraits painted for the Drummond family at Hawthornden. Their superb quality (in many ways superior to the larger portraits) suggests the hand of David himself or a close associate.

Plate 26

COSMO ALEXANDER (1724-1772) *Prince Charles Edward Stuart* oil on canvas 29 x 30 inches signed and dated 1752 (lower left)

Exhibited: Edinburgh, *Exhibition of Scottish National Portraits*, 1884 (No.489)

This is one of a set of four portraits of members of the exiled Stuart Royal Family painted in 1748-52. Alexander was a committed Jacobite who had fled to the Continent in 1746 where he painted a number of prominent Jacobite exiles. Prince Charles's whereabouts in the 1750-55 period are unclear and so it cannot be said for certain that this was painted from life, although it would seem likely. Despite some weaknesses in the drawing and overall composition, this appears to be a remarkably accurate portrait, the facial features bearing close comparison with Lemoyne's 1746 bust.

Plate 27

JEAN-BAPTISTE LEMOYNE (1704-1778) *Prince Charles Edward Stuart* plaster Height: 19½ inches

Sculpted shortly after his return from Scotland in 1746, this is considered the best likeness produced of the Prince. Plaster casts of the bust were distributed widely and were even sold covertly in London.

Plate 28

after SIR ROBERT STRANGE (1721-1792) *Prince Charles Edward Stuart* oil on canvas 29 x 24½ inches

In the 1746-60 period, a large number of copies of portraits of Prince Charles were painted showing the sitter dressed in tartan, some possibly painted in Scotland, but most probably the work of exiled Jacobite artists on the Continent. Many were derived from the portrait drawn by Robert Strange in 1745 (plate 31) and these were to become the model for his appearance on glasses, medals and miniatures.

Although Charles occasionally wore Highland dress during the campaigns of 1745-6, it was only in the years after the Uprising and partly through the medium of the portraits, that the mythology developed of Charles as a quintessentially Scottish hero, a semi-nationalist ideology that was revived in the 19th century and has been sustained since.

Plate 29

JAMES FERGUSON (1710-1776) *Prince Charles Edward Stuart, c.1745* pencil on paper Height: 2¼ inches

Ferguson, a well-established Aberdonian miniaturist, was one of the few Scottish artists to depict Prince Charles, although it is uncertain whether he ever actually saw the Prince. It is an unusual portrait in that it does not show the characteristic sash of the Order of the Garter.

Plate 30

CONTINENTAL SCHOOL mid 18th Century *Prince Charles Edward in Tartan* oil on canvas 29 x 24 inches

The origins of the so-called 'Harlequin' portraits of Prince Charles are obscure. A number exist, all painted to the same dimensions, differing only slightly in colour and details of costume. The peculiar rendering of the tartan suit suggests that the artist had no first hand experience of the fabric and the distinctive Roman style of the fortifications in the background might indicate an Italian hand.

Plate 31

SIR ROBERT STRANGE (1721-1792) *Prince Charles Edward Stuart* copper engraving 10 x 7 inches

Strange, who originally came from Orkney, was to make his reputation with this image. It is derived from a mezzotint that he produced while the Prince was resident at Holyrood and was considered a good likeness. Strange fought at Culloden and fled to France where he produced this more elaborate engraving, bearing a quotation from Virgil's *Georgics* - '*everso missus succurrere seclo*' - 'sent to help a ruined age'.

Strange was later reconciled to the Hanoverian monarchy and received a knighthood for his engravings of the Royal family.

- Jacobite Works of Art -

Plate 32

after LOUIS TOCQUE (1696-1772) (engraved by J.G. Wille) *Prince Charles Edward Stuart* copper engraving 17½ x 12 inches

This print is taken from a portrait that was commissioned by the Duchess de Montbazon in 1747 but which is now lost. It is probably the finest portrait engraving of the Prince.

Plate 33

after ALLAN RAMSAY (1713-1784) (engraved by James McArdell) *Flora MacDonald* mezzotint 12¾ x 8¾ inches

Plate 34

after THOMAS HUDSON (1701-1779) (engraved by J. Faber) *Flora MacDonald* mezzotint 12 x 10 inches

Flora MacDonald enjoyed great celebrity for the romantic part she played in the 1745 and was courted by London society after her release from the Tower in 1747. Ramsay painted her in 1749 and the original now hangs in the Ashmolean Museum. The profusion of white roses makes the sitter's allegiance clearly apparent.

Hudson's extremely romanticised portrayal is even less subtle, with the Jacobite heroine, in the garb of a shepherdess, gesturing at a miniature of Charles, while in the background is shown the boat in which she accompanied the Prince to safety. The 'cult' of Flora MacDonald in the post-1745 period seemed to bear no relationship to serious Jacobite sympathies, rather showing how quickly the events of the period had entered popular mythology.

Plate 35

after THOMAS HUDSON (1701-1779) (engraved by J. Faber) *Benn's Club of Aldermen* mezzotint 15 x 21 inches

This print of one of Hudson's most celebrated group compositions shows the members of a Jacobite Club about to enjoy a glass of wine. The six members of a 'well known society of worthy aldermen' allied themselves to the Jacobite Cause in 1745 and were the chief contacts in the City of London for the Jacobite MP, Sir Watkins William Wynn.

On their exposure in 1746 they fled to the Isle of Wight and the letter on the floor, from Sir Watkins, suggests they may have just heard the news that they were not to be prosecuted. From left to right the aldermen are Thomas Rawlinson of the Grocers Company, Robert Alsop of the Ironmongers, Edward Ironside of the Goldsmiths, Henry Marshall of the Drapers, William Benn of the Fletchers (who wears a tartan waistcoat to indicate his sympathies) and John Blachford of the Goldsmiths. Standing is Blachford's brother who is serving as butler to the group.

It is clubs such as this which would have been the main customers for engraved Jacobite drinking glasses.

Plate 36

attributed to COSMO ALEXANDER (1724-1772) *A Jacobite Lady with a White Rose - possibly Miss Jenny Cameron* oil on canvas 19 x 17 inches

The identity of 'Jenny Cameron' putative mistress of Bonnie Prince Charlie has long been disputed. It has been suggested that she is Jenny Cameron of Glendessary who accompanied her brother to Glenfinnan to watch the raising of the Jacobite standard. Reports of her striking appearance reached the London anti-Jacobite writers who declared she was mistress of the Prince and described her wearing extraordinary tartan costumes.

Another 'Jenny Cameron', an Edinburgh milliner, was taken prisoner by the Duke of Cumberland, and on her release did nothing to dispel the idea that she was the Prince's mistress, rightly seeing it as a way of improving her business.

Plate 37

A SELECTION OF MEDALS 1689-1720

a) *James II & VII, his wife and heir flee from England and are received by France 1689* bronze 1½ inches by I. Mauger
b) *Prince James Edward Stuart promoted as successor to James II & VII 1699* silver 1⅜ inches by Norbert Roettier
c) *The Jacobite Invasion of 1708 is repulsed - a pro-Hanoverian medal* by George Hautsch silver 1½ inches
d) *The Birth of Prince Charles Edward Stuart 1720* bronze gilt 1⅝ inches by Ottone Hamerani

Plate 38

A SELECTION OF MEDALS 1749-1772

a) *The 1745 - Commemorative Medals - A Highlander and, on the reverse, a Jacobite Rose 1749* bronze/bronze gilt 1⅛ inches maker unknown
b) *A Highlander Medal, c.1750* copper 2 inches by Thomas Pingo
c) *The Oak Society Medal, 1750, possibly commemorating an incognito visit by Prince Charles to London* silver/copper 1⅜ inches by Charles Norbert Roettier and Thomas Pingo
d) *A Royal Touch Piece, Charles III* silver ¾ inch by Ferdinando Hammerani
e) *The Marriage of Charles III and Louise of Stolberg 1772* silver 1¼ inches by Ferdinando Hammerani

Both the Hanoverian and Jacobite Courts produced large quantities of propaganda medals celebrating events and individuals to reinforce their claims to legitimacy. Craftsmen, such as the Roettier and Hammerani families, worked almost full-time on such commissions. The medals share much of the imagery and symbolism that is to be found on Jacobite drinking glasses and were a more readily concealable way of demonstrating loyalty. 'Touch pieces' which were given to those 'touched' by the King to cure the 'Royal Malady' were only produced by the Jacobites suggesting, perhaps, that they had more confidence in the divine right of their Kingship.

The Drambuie Collection
of
Scottish Paintings

Plate 39

John Phillip (1817-1867)
A Scotch Roadside Inn, 1850

oil on board 13½ x 17½ inches
signed, dated and inscribed (bottom right)

Phillip, an Aberdeen artist, is best known for his elaborate and popular scenes of Spanish life. In his early career, however, much under the influence of David Wilkie and Edwin Landseer, he painted a series of fluid and accomplished sketches of Highland life. In this example, a Highland huntsman is shown stopping at a wayside inn. The advertisment above the door and the distinctive shape of the glass suggest that wine, rather than whisky or a liqueur, is his preferred tipple.

- Scottish Paintings -

The history of painting in Scotland is relatively short compared to the long artistic traditions of other European countries. The Scottish School, however, is a unique one with attributes and qualities that set it apart, not only from its continental equivalents, but from England, whose cultural domination has never extended as far as its political supremacy.

In recent years, art historians have done much to re-evaluate Scottish art and demonstrate the unique qualities of some of its practitioners. Artists, of whom little was known thirty years ago, have been restored to prominence and it has been convincingly established that painters of the highest order flourished in Scotland, independently and without recourse to the practices or traditions of English art.

Scottish art now enjoys greater respect and popular admiration than it has ever done before. The Drambuie Collection of Scottish Paintings reflects some of the qualities that make Scottish painting distinctive and appealing and the selection illustrated here is typical of the broad range of style and subject-matter that characterise the nation's art. The earliest paintings in the Collection date from the beginning of the 19th century when Scottish artists began to realise that there was a cultured and appreciative audience within their own country and that it was no longer necessary to suffer exile in the south, or draw on foreign traditions, to make a reputation. The largest part of the Collection is of works from the mid to late 19th century, a 'golden age' of Scottish painting when a gifted generation of Edinburgh-trained artists established the realities of a true 'Scottish School of Painting'. The later works, from the 1890s to the 1930s, show Scottish artists becoming cosmopolitan, taking on the avant-garde ideas of the European Schools and re-working them into a uniquely Scottish idiom.

Inevitably, the portrayal of landscape has always been a significant part of Scottish painting. However, it was not until the late 18th and early 19th centuries, that artists and travellers began to appreciate the attractions of the Scottish landscape. Under the guidance of the Romantic poets and writers, the mountains and torrents of the Highlands began to be seen not as hindrances to travel or cultivation, but as wonderful examples of the picturesque and the sublime, evoking awe and encouraging contemplation. The artist who was to capture this essence and in so doing receive the honorary title 'the father of Scottish landscape painting' was the Edinburgh painter, Alexander Nasmyth.

Nasmyth was a true Enlightenment figure: philosopher, architect, engineer, artist and friend of the poet, Burns, with whom he shared a radical political outlook. This last fact may have lost Nasmyth important aristocratic portrait commissions and forced him to paint landscapes. If so it was a happy misfortune, for Nasmyth approached landscape with an exquisite sensibility, seeing in it a reflection of man's essential relationship with nature. A natural teacher, Nasmyth set up a school and his influence on the rising generation of artists was immense.

His own children were, in many ways, his finest pupils. Of his eleven offspring, eight became artists of accomplishment. *A Highland Loch* and *A View of the Tay* by Jane and Charlotte Nasmyth, respectively, (*Plates 40, 41*) are delightful examples of the Nasmyth interpretation of landscape combining an extreme sensitivity to natural light and atmosphere, while at the same time imposing a classical, even logical, order to the view.

By the mid-19th century, landscape painters had begun to move away from Nasmyth's approach and treat more dramatic effects of weather and terrain. Horatio McCulloch and Sam Bough became masters of vertiginous heights and crashing storms. Keeley Halswelle, a close associate of McCulloch contributed a quintessential example to the genre with his *Newhaven* of 1863 (*Plate 43*) in which soaring, luridly coloured cloud effects, dwarf and dominate the trudging fisher folk. A similarly scaled piece by Joseph Adam and his son (*Plate 42*) manages also to demonstrate the Scottish love of animal painting, here set against a vast and inhospitable mountain-scape.

A final flowering of this landscape tradition appeared in the work of Joseph Farquharson who was, in many ways, close to the spirit of Nasmyth in his observation of the fine nuances of atmosphere and the humanity and inhumanities of the landscape. Settled for many years at Finzean in Aberdeenshire, Farquharson developed a dazzling technical accomplishment in his painting of snow, frost and the red glow of the winter sun. Two sketches (*Plates 47, 48*), effortlessly painted, sum up his command of the medium and his ability to evoke an effect of light that is so true to the Scottish winter.

Alexander Nasmyth's art school was the first attempt to establish a teaching tradition indigenous to Scotland. Too often Scottish painters were drawn to London, frustrated by the inadequacy of training provisions in their native land. The twenty year old David Wilkie fled south in 1805 and established a reputation virtually overnight with his intuitive and unaffected depictions of Scottish village life. Fêted as the 'Scottish Teniers', he encouraged his compatriots to migrate to London, arguing that an independent presence of Scots artists in the great metropolis would more readily encourage a 'native art' than unrewarded efforts in the provinces.

Alas, the pressures were too great and even Wilkie, possibly the most admired Scottish artist ever, suffered a breakdown in 1825 and a subsequent deterioration in the quality of his work. Few of those fellow countrymen who heard his call flourished, with the possible exception of Thomas Faed who more readily adapted his art to the changeable *mores* of English taste. Others, such as the Dundonian, William Simson (*Plate 1*), failed to live up to early expectations and died young, their promise unfulfilled.

Robert Scott Lauder, a contemporary of Simson, moved to London in 1838. His ambition was to paint great canvasses of historical scenes, then considered the highest achievement of art, superior to landscape, genre or portraiture. His work in the field was praised (*Plate 49*) and Lauder was encouraged to enter a competition in 1847 to paint murals for the newly re-built Houses of Parliament, a potential culmination to his career. His proposals were rejected and, disillusioned, Lauder decided to return to Edinburgh and take up a post as Master of the Trustees' Academy. In the next nine years he was to oversee the emergence of a true 'Scottish School of Painting'.

Established in the early years of the century, the Trustees' Academy had made sporadic inroads into the teaching of the fine arts in Scotland. Under Lauder it took on a revitalised role and the energy and commitment of its Master staunched the flow of native talent to England. The artists Lauder taught from 1852-61 dominated Scottish art for the rest of the century: Robert Herdman, George Chalmers, John Pettie, Peter Graham, William McTaggart, John Burr, William Quiller Orchardson, to name but a handful. Lauder enthused and goaded; he constantly emphasised the importance of fine draughtsmanship and, in a move entirely contradictory to existing practice, encouraged students to use paints from the earliest opportunity.

Critics, in Scotland and England, soon noted the effects of Lauder's teaching: a concern for colour (*Plates 51, 55*) and, above all, an awareness of the tactile qualities of paint and surface (*Plates 52, 53, 59*). The dominance, in England, of the theorising of John Ruskin and the works of the Pre-Raphaelites and the academic painters which emphasised quality of 'finish' and exacting verisimilitude, meant the paintings of Lauder's pupils were greeted with a combination of astonishment and acclaim. But popular appreciation was wholehearted and for the first time Scottish artists were enjoying a nation-wide reputation without having to repudiate their native soil.

Some of course did move to London, but entered artistic circles there at the highest level, and continued to maintain a close network with their Scottish peers. They enjoyed the accolades of the great exhibiting institutions and Orchardson, knighted in 1907, is buried in St. Paul's Cathedral. His shimmering essay in tone and light, *Dolce far Niente (Plate 53)*, is a particular gem of the collection and clearly shows the immense impact his work had on artists as diverse as Whistler and Sickert.

The subject matter of these artists is diverse, ranging from intimate portrait studies, to landscapes and fully-developed history paintings. The most fascinating treatment of subject, however, was developed in the hands of William McTaggart who, quite independently, arrived at a proto-Impressionist way of breaking down the elements of a picture into its essential constituents. His early work is characterised by a surprising lightness of touch (*Plate 58*), reflecting the allusiveness of his subject, his concern with the transient sensations of childhood. By the 1880s, he was painting out of doors, building up images with deft flicks of paint, endeavouring to encapsulate the landscape as an effect of highlights and shadows (*Plate 59*) Although he visited Paris, McTaggart claimed to be unaware of the innovations of the Impressionists, and his late work is an extraordinary expression of individual application. Like Constable seventy years earlier, he demonstrated how the British landscape is so ineffably bound up with light, weather and atmospheric effect.

By the 1880s, Scottish painters had the confidence to work on an international stage. A disdain of the undoubtedly stale approaches of the teaching academies drew artists to Paris where, in the *ateliers*, academic masters, such as Bougereau, instilled the qualities of life drawing. But at weekends and during holidays, the young painters turned to the avant-garde, artists such as Bastien-Lepage and his associates of the Barbizon School, who encouraged painting in the open air and, above all, painting that was 'true to life'.

These ideas were rapidly assimilated and Scottish artists sought out equivalent themes within their local environments. William Darling McKay became part of a group based in East Linton, outside Edinburgh, who modelled themselves on the Barbizon painters and portrayed the harsh life of the manual worker (*Plate 61*). Others sought inspiration from Dutch prototypes and the painters of the 'Hague School' who were much collected in Scotland. Robert Gemmell Hutchison became a master of this sort of loose naturalism, tinged with sentimentality. However, his *Village Carnival* of 1898 (*Plate 62*) is a quite exceptional *tour de force* clearly intended to make his reputation as an artist able to command an intricate and demanding composition. While such paintings are an obvious continuation of the Wilkie tradition of genre they also show how Scots artists at this time often preferred to leaven the realities of life with a touch of levity or humour.

With the emergence of a more varied and cosmopolitan approach to painting in Scotland, the artistic focus shifted from Edinburgh to Glasgow. A group of artists appeared who disdained the stuffiness of the Royal Scottish Academy and decided to exhibit in the more radical institutions, such as the Glasgow Institute and the New English Art Club. They became known as the 'Glasgow Boys' and were the most cohesive body of Scottish painters to appear since Lauder's days in the 1850s

Not that there was much obvious unity to their work. Some of their number, such as James Guthrie and E.A. Walton, adhered closely to Barbizon principles, but others travelled further afield for inspiration. In 1891 John Lavery, who was of Irish birth, travelled to France and Spain, where, much influenced by the painting of Edouard Manet, he painted a series of jewel-like sketches (*Plate 64*), anticipating the technical mastery and bravura handling of paint that were to characterise his later career as portrait painter. The following year, George Henry and Edward Hornel visited Japan and, for the latter in particular, this was to be a crucial formative influence. The paintings executed after his return (*Plate 63*) demonstrate an instinctive feeling for space and the limitations and possibilities of the restricted picture plane.

Scottish art at the dawn of the 20th century had perhaps, in its reliance on European, particularly French, innovation, lost some of the freshness and vigour of fifty years previously. However, artists continued to adapt ideas within a distinctive Scottish sensibility and it is this that characterises the paintings of the period - a constant re-working of Continental ideas into a Scottish idiom.

No group displays this tendency more clearly than the 'Scottish Colourists' who inherited the avant-garde mantle from the 'Glasgow Boys'. While the 'Boys' had sought inspiration in the muted palettes of Bastien-Lepage and Corot , the Colourists were galvanised by the bold colours of the 'Fauves' the 'Wild Beasts ' of Parisian art. The 1906 Fauve exhibition had an immediate impact on two of the Colourists - Peploe and Fergusson - and their ideas soon passed to the other two members of the group - Cadell and Hunter. Colour, rather than light or texture, became the crucial constituent of a painting, the way that structure could be imposed on the subject-matter.

But the traditionally Scottish nature of the Colourists' subjects - still-life, interiors, landscape - muted the more extreme development of the French colour theories and by the 1920s their paintings are assured re-workings of accessible themes. The two most consistent members of the group are represented by outstanding examples in the collection. Samuel John Peploe's *Still Life with Japanese Jar and Roses* (*Plate 67*) combines hot and quite startling colours in an arrangement that, while re-calling the modernity of Art Deco, is surprisingly traditional in its intention. At the other extreme, Francis Cadell's *Interior* (*Plate 66*) of the 1930s is an icy cool essay in angles and spaces, with a subtle domination of blue. His earlier *Iona - the East Bay* (*Plate 65*) is a quintessential Colourist work; a traditional landscape view, but painted with the most saturated colours, enhanced by the absorbent ground underneath the paint. Because of the strength of its colours, the island of Iona attracted the Colourists and their emulators. But, at the end of the day, Cadell's *Iona* is a logical and restrained rendition of the Scottish landscape and could well have found favour with Nasmyth.

The impact of the Colourists on the succeeding generation was low-key, which might surprise those who hold them in such esteem today. Already, with the constant change and speeding up of innovation that so characterises art in the 20th century, another fashion was in vogue. The artistic mantle returned to Edinburgh and her College of Art was to hold sway until well after the War. The young William Mactaggart (grand-son of the pupil of Lauder) was a typical product and his *Castle in the Snow* (*Plate 68*), one of his finest early works, shows the direction of change. The emphasis is not only on colour but the liquid possibilities of the paint itself, which is applied with a sensitivity to its tactile, visual qualities as a medium. '*Belle Peinture*' was the phrase coined to describe the works of the 'Edinburgh School' signifying their concern with the actual act of painting as being of greatest significance, a refreshingly down-to-earth view that has typified the outlook of Scottish painters through many generations.

The hundred and fifty years of painting tradition encompassed by the Drambuie Collection saw Scottish artists emerge from the shadow of the English School and establish an individual presence on the international stage. The paintings in the Collection reflect the qualities of the Scots painters who persevered in their commitment to a truly 'national' school of painting. The small selection illustrated here shows how much Scottish painting is an integral part of the heritage of modern Scotland.

Further Reading:

Duncan MacMillan, *Scottish Painting 1460-1990*, Mainstream, 1990

Plate 40

Jane Nasmyth (1788-1867)
A Highland Loch

Plate 41

Charlotte Nasmyth (1804-1866)
A View from Elcho Castle, looking towards Ben Lawers

Plate 42

Joseph Adam (fl.1858-1880) & Joseph Denovan Adam (1842-1896)
Highland Cattle with a Collie

Plate 43

Keeley Halswelle (1832-1891)
Newhaven, Firth of Forth, Sunset

Plate 44

James Cassie (1819-1879)
The Firth of Forth from the Mouth of the Almond

Plate 45

Sir William Fettes Douglas (1822-1891)
Nocturne

Plate 46

Sir William Fettes Douglas (1822-1891)
The Prisoner

Plate 47

Joseph Farquharson (1846-1935)
Sheep in a Winter Landscape, Evening

Plate 48

Joseph Farquharson (1846-1935)
Sheep in the Snow

Plate 49

Robert Scott Lauder (1803-1869)
The Penance of Jane Shore

Plate 50

John Burr (1831-1893)
The Vintner

Plate 51

Robert Herdman (1828-1888)
Dressing for a Charade: The Children of Patrick Allan Fraser

Plate 52

John Pettie (1839-1893)
In the Costume of the XVII Century

Plate 53

Sir William Quiller Orchardson (1832-1910)
Dolce far Niente

Plate 54

Peter Graham (1836-1921)
Seagulls and Gannets

Plate 55

John MacWhirter (1839-1911)
Genoa

Plate 56

William McTaggart (1835-1910)
Portrait Study

Plate 57

William McTaggart (1835-1910)
Study for 'Dora'

Plate 58

William McTaggart (1835-1910)
Playmates

Plate 59

William McTaggart (1835-1910)
Natural Harbour, Cockenzie

Plate 60

Sir David Murray (1849-1933)
Fieldworkers, Holland

Plate 61

William Darling McKay (1844-1924)
Stonebreakers

Plate 62

Robert Gemmell Hutchison (1855-1936)
The Village Carnival: Hi! Hi!! Hi!!!

Plate 63

Edward Atkinson Hornel (1864-1933)
The Lily Pond

Plate 64

Sir John Lavery (1856-1941)
El Embiste

Plate 65

Francis Campbell Boileau Cadell (1883-1937)
Iona - The East Bay, 1928

76

Plate 66

Francis Campbell Boileau Cadell (1883-1937)
Interior - 30 Regent Terrace

Plate 67

Samuel John Peploe (1871-1935)
Still Life with Japanese Jar and Roses

Plate 68

Sir William Mactaggart (1903-1981)
The Castle in the Snow

- Scottish Paintings -

Plate 40

JANE NASMYTH (1788-1867) *A Highland Lochside* oil on canvas 17½ x 23½ inches signed and dated 1847 (bottom left)

The eldest of Alexander Nasmyth's children, Jane showed a precocious talent and from an early age assisted her father in his York Place art school. Endeavouring to teach his pupils (drawn from the young gentry and well-to-do ladies of Edinburgh) the qualities of the picturesque and the sublime in the Scottish landscape, Nasmyth had his daughter take parties on extended sketching trips around Arthur's Seat, an unusual and innovative approach in an age when most teaching was done in the studio.

Jane Nasmyth usually painted her landscapes from life, but in this case the scene may be imaginary, a sort of *capriccio* pastoral, reminiscent of the work of Claude Lorrain, chief inspiration for a whole generation of landscape painters. The painting, unusually, is signed; problems of attribution occur frequently with the Nasmyth family and Jane's paintings are often confused with those of her sister, Barbara.

Plate 41

CHARLOTTE NASMYTH (1804-1866) *A View from Elcho Castle, looking towards Ben Lawers* oil on canvas 18 x 24 inches

Born at 47 York Place, Edinburgh, Charlotte was the youngest and most prolific of Alexander Nasmyth's daughters. She taught at her father's art school and always stayed true to his precepts regarding the composition of the picturesque landscape, clearly apparent here, with the trees framing the scene, the road and river drawing the eye inwards, and the boats and figures giving scale to the whole

Plate 42

JOSEPH ADAM (fl.1858-1880) & JOSEPH DENOVAN ADAM (1842-1896) *Highland Cattle with a Collie* oil on canvas 35 x 58 inches signed with initials (lower right)

Denovan Adam kept a farm near Stirling where he encouraged a small group of local animal painters. It is likely that his father, who specialised in landscape, painted the backdrop of this scene, giving the composition a far more grandiose (and, indeed, successful) air than is normal in the younger artist's pictures. Relatively sophisticated paintings of this sort are the culmination of a long tradition of naive and primitive animal painting in Scotland, characterised by artists such as Howe of Skirling, Alexander Carse and Walter Geikie.

Plate 43

KEELEY HALSWELLE RSA (1832-1891) *Newhaven, Firth of Forth, Sunset* oil on canvas 30 x 52 inches signed and inscribed with title on stretcher

Exhibited: Royal Scottish Academy, 1863 (No.266)

Halswelle, an Edinburgh artist, is best known for his depictions of Italian subjects from the 1870s and 80s. But prior to that, inspired by his teacher, Horatio McCulloch, he had painted a highly accomplished series of genre and landscape paintings of the East Coast fishing villages of Scotland, of which this is one of the more melodramatic.

Plate 44

JAMES CASSIE RSA RSW (1819-1879) *The Firth of Forth from the Mouth of the Almond* oil on canvas 15½ x 30 inches signed and dated '64 (bottom right)

Exhibited: Royal Scottish Academy, 1865 (No. 704)

An Aberdeen-shire painter, Cassie was much influenced by the Pre-Raphaelites and their concern for meticulous observation of nature. A serious injury in his youth restricted his painting forays to the lowlands of the East Coast.

Plates 45 & 46

SIR WILLIAM FETTES DOUGLAS PRSA (1822-1891) *The Prisoner* oil on panel 6 x 5 inches signed with initials and dated 1873 (top right) *Nocturne* oil on panel 6 x 5 inches

Like the Pre-Raphaelite painters who inspired him, Fettes Douglas was obsessed with painting the minutiae of interiors and historical scenes. A largely self-taught painter, he was also an antiquarian and collector and it is often his cherished possessions that are the chief subjects of his paintings.

In this pair of charming panels of the 1870s, the ostensible subjects - the prisoner and the musician - are very much in the background, barely revealed behind a cluttered, but exquisitely painted, still-life.

Plates 47 & 48

JOSEPH FARQUHARSON RA (1846-1935) *Sheep in a Winter Landscape, Evening* oil on canvas 12 x 18 inches signed (bottom left) *Sheep in the Snow* oil on canvas 12 x 18 inches signed (bottom left)

Although part of the earliest generation of Scottish painters to train in Paris (in the 1880s) Farquharson's reputation was made with the series of evocative evening snowscapes he painted over many years in the neighbourhood of Finzean in Aberdeenshire. Enduringly popular, their regular appearance on the walls of the Royal Academy brought him great celebrity.

- Scottish Paintings -

Plate 49

ROBERT SCOTT LAUDER RSA (1803-1869)
The Penance of Jane Shore oil on canvas 53 x
71 inches signed and indistinctly inscribed
(verso)

Exhibited: Royal Scottish Academy, 1850 (No.160)

Jane Shore was the mistress of Edward IV, but after
his death his successor, Richard III, in an act of spite,
forced the Bishop of London to make her walk the
streets of London in penance, carrying a taper and
dressed only in her kirtle. This story, popularised in
a play by Nicholas Rowe, was an ideal subject for
Lauder, combining historical costume, an elaborate
figure composition and a high degree of pathos. This
latter aspect was particularly marked by the critic of
the *Art Journal* who wrote of *"the attitude of deep
sorrow and humiliation...which is as beautifully
conceived as it is exquisitely rendered"*.

Plate 50

JOHN BURR ROI ARWS 1831-1893 *The
Vintner* oil on canvas 26 x 38 inches signed and
dated 1886 (lower right)

Like so many of Robert Scott Lauder's most talented
pupils of the 1850s, John Burr went on to achieve
great success in London. His gentle scenes of
domestic and local life, occasionally enlivened by
incidental or humorous details had a ready appeal.
This example is unusually ambitious in the
complexity of the figural composition, but shares
with other works the pastel colours and tonal
subtleties he generally favoured.

Plate 51

ROBERT HERDMAN RSA RSW (1828-1888)
*Dressing for a Charade: The Children of
Patrick Allan Fraser* oil on canvas 15 x 18
inches signed and dated 1886 (bottom right)

Exhibited: Royal Scottish Academy, 1886 (No.268)
Illustrated: Lindsay Errington, *Robert Herdman*,
National Galleries of Scotland, Scottish Masters
Series, 1988, p.26

Although taught by Lauder, Herdman was equally
influenced by the Pre-Raphaelitism of John Everett
Millais, who regularly visited Scotland from the
1860s. So, unlike many of his Scots contemporaries,
Herdman was always concerned with intense
colours, exacting brushwork and 'finish'.
Patrick Allan Fraser was one of the leading patrons
of Scottish art and his home, Hospitalfield (which
was probably the setting for this painting), still
flourishes as an art school today.

Plate 52

JOHN PETTIE RA HRSA (1839-1893) *In the
Costume of the XVII Century* oil on canvas
31 x 23 inches signed and dated 1875 (bottom
left)

Exhibited: Royal Scottish Academy, 1877 (No.87)

This bravura portrait of his friend, G.F. White, is
typical of Pettie and his circle who constantly
sketched and painted one another. Pettie had moved
to London with Orchardson in the 1870s and swiftly
established a reputation as a painter of historical
subjects, his sure handling of costume particularly
evident in this work, which shows obvious debts to
the paintings of Hals and Rembrandt.

Plate 53

SIR WILLIAM QUILLER ORCHARDSON
RA HRSA (1832-1910) *Dolce far Niente* oil on
canvas 29 x 39 inches signed and dated '72
(bottom right)

Of all Robert Scott Lauder's pupils of the 1850s,
Orchardson achieved the greatest success. Lauded
and admired by the British public he received the
ultimate accolade after his death when he was buried
in St. Paul's Cathedral. His history, society and
drawing-room paintings were immensely popular,
combining a fluid style, clever composition and
intriguing narrative twists. However, in his more
intimate paintings, such as *Dolce far Niente*, he adds
an extra dimension, a more subtle interplay of light
and pattern, which eminently suits his use of thin
layers of transparent oil paint.
Possibly portraying his wife, who he had married
recently, this painting also shows the growing
obsession with things Japanese and their essentially
decorative qualities. Unlike so many of his pictures,
such works are primarily aesthetic compositions,
'arrangements', and as such, it has been suggested,
may have had a great influence on Whistler.

Plate 54

PETER GRAHAM HRA ARSA (1836-1921)
Seagulls and Gannets oil on canvas 54 x 72
inches signed and dated 1900 (bottom right)

Exhibited: (possibly) Royal Academy, 1900 (No.
206) as *Ocean's surge, white as the sea-bird's wing*

After his training at the Trustee's Academy, Graham
made a stunning debut at the Royal Academy of
1862 with *A Spate in the Highlands*. Like his
contemporary, John MacWhirter, Graham
concentrated on depicting the remote Highlands, in
particular the rugged coastlines, which suited his
fluid loose brushwork and command of dizzy
perspectives.

Plate 55

JOHN MacWHIRTER RA HRSA RSW (1839-1911) *Genoa* oil on canvas 17½ x 30 inches signed (bottom right)

Like Peter Graham, MacWhirter devoted himself exclusively to landscape painting, both in Scotland and during his extensive trips to the Continent. He painted this particular scene, taken from his hotel window, many times on his visit to Genoa in 1904, anxious to capture the rapidly fading afterglow, which he described as "one of the most lovely effects in nature".

Plate 56

WILLIAM McTAGGART RSA (1835-1910) *Portrait Study, possibly the artist's brother, Duncan* oil on board 10 x 8 inches signed (bottom right)

Exhibited: National Galleries of Scotland, *William McTaggart*, 1989 (No.5)
Literature: James L. Caw, *William McTaggart*, Glasgow, 1917, p.222

Probably painted quite early in the artist's career, c.1860. The suggested identity of the sitter is by no means certain, although at this period Duncan was writing endless letters to his more successful brother requesting loans and may often have visited in person.

Plate 57

WILLIAM McTAGGART RSA (1835-1910) *Study for 'Dora'* oil on canvas 10 x 8 inches signed and dated 1866 (lower left)

Exhibited: Glasgow, 'East End Exhibition', 1891
Literature: James L. Caw, *William McTaggart*, Glasgow, 1917, p.46-47, 229; Lindsay Errington, *William McTaggart*, Edinburgh, 1989, pp.40-43

This study for McTaggart's major diploma piece of 1868 shows the original conception of the picture: a twilight scene emphasising the melancholy contrast between adult experience and childish innocence. But McTaggart was to repaint the larger work, making it lighter and brighter, marking, as Lindsay Errington has suggested, "a decision in favour of lightness and space which was to mark all his later work"
This study, therefore, comes at a seminal stage in his artistic development, when a significant break with the Pre-Raphaelite influences of his early years was to enable McTaggart to experiment with open brushwork and broader effects.

Plate 58

WILLIAM McTAGGART RSA (1835-1910) *Playmates* oil on canvas 14¾ x 19¾ inches signed and dated 1867 (bottom right)

Possibly a finished study for the painting exhibited at The Royal Scottish Academy in 1867, this painting is characteristic of all McTaggart's works of the late 1860s, dwelling on the innocence of children and their spontaneous affinity with nature.

Plate 59

WILLIAM McTAGGART RSA (1835-1910) *Natural Harbour, Cockenzie* oil on canvas 34 x 37 inches signed (lower centre)

Literature: James L. Caw, *William McTaggart*, Glasgow, 1917, pp.178, 267

A quintessential painting of McTaggart's late period. With a pale priming he builds up the image using a very limited tonal range, the shadows virtually transparent, only the highlights opaque, effortlessly creating a sense of silvery calm with the most economic means. As in nearly all the pictures of this period, the figures are almost subsumed into the rocks, becoming part of the overall design.

Plate 60

SIR DAVID MURRAY RA HRSA (1849-1933) *Fieldworkers, Holland* oil on canvas 19 x 37 inches signed (bottom right)

Like almost all his contemporaries, Murray looked to the Continent for inspiration, particularly the French painters of the Barbizon School and their advocacy of *plein-air* painting, vigorous brushwork and subject-matter drawn from everyday life. Murray visited Holland frequently in the 1880s and probably painted this painting during one of these trips, attracted no doubt by the picturesque attributes of the rural workers and the flat, broad landscape so suited to a horizontal picture plain.

Plate 61

WILLIAM DARLING McKAY RSA (1844-1924) *Stonebreakers, East Lothian* oil on canvas 19 x 27 inches signed (bottom left)

Exhibited: Royal Scottish Academy, 1877 (No.236)

Born in Gifford, East Lothian, McKay trained at the Trustees Academy in Edinburgh and was soon to associate himself with a group of artists who painted in and around the village of East Linton. Emulating the Barbizon painters, they worked in the open air and disdained obviously picturesque subject matter. The harsh life of the stonebreaker would have had an immediate appeal and McKay portrays the rigours of their work (even the eye-shields to protect from flying stones) with uncompromising realism.

- Scottish Paintings -

Plate 62

ROBERT GEMMELL HUTCHISON RSA RSW (1855-1936) *The Village Carnival: Hi! Hi!! Hi!!!* oil on canvas 45 x 62 inches signed (bottom centre)

Exhibited: Royal Scottish Academy, 1898 (No.441)

Hutchison is best known for his small-scale, loosely painted depictions of children at the seashore and in interiors and in such works shows clear debts to contemporaries like William McTaggart and the painters of the popular 'Hague School' However, in this major exhibition piece of the 1890s he attempted something quite different and successfully carried off a daring and elaborate composition. A number of his favourite models of the period appear in the painting, notably the old man and the child with the pink hood to the right of the scene. *The Village Carnival* was probably Hutchison's response to the large-scale paintings of the Newlyn School, especially Stanhope Forbes, which were receiving critical acclaim in London at this time and is a remarkably successful essay in this sort of sentimental realism.

Plate 63

EDWARD ATKINSON HORNEL (1864-1933) *The Lily Pond* oil on canvas 37 x 19 inches signed and dated 1900 (bottom right)

Hornel was one of the 'Glasgow Boys' who were at the forefront of artistic innovation in Scotland in the 1880s and 1890s. His concern for the decorative qualities of painting became predominant after a visit to Japan in 1892 and this painting shows him at the height of his powers before a tendency to repetitive and maudlin subject matter became apparent, blighting the paintings of his later career.

Plate 64

SIR JOHN LAVERY RA RSA RHA (1856-1941) *El Embiste* oil on canvas, laid down on card 8¼ x 4¾ inches signed and dated 1892

Lavery visited Spain and North Africa in 1891/2 and, like his fellow Glasgow School painter, Joseph Crawhall, was fascinated by the bull-fight, later commenting "it is the moving colour that attracts me at this cruel sport". The technique is unusual - building up the image with translucent dark tones and then adding opaque highlights - similar to that employed by Manet, emphasising the extraordinary versatility of Lavery at this early stage in his career.

Plate 65

FRANCIS CAMPBELL BOILEAU CADELL (1883-1937) *Iona - The East Bay, 1928* oil on canvas 20 x 30 inches signed (bottom left)

Cadell first visited Iona in 1912 and returned there frequently over the next twenty years, often accompanied by fellow Colourist, S.J. Peploe. He developed a technique of using an absorbent white ground which intensified the blues and aquamarines, just as the white sands of Iona affect the sea and rocks.

Plate 66

FRANCIS CAMPBELL BOILEAU CADELL (1883-1937) *Interior - 30 Regent Terrace* oil on canvas 24 x 20 inches signed (bottom left) inscribed with title (verso)

Literature: Tom Hewlett, *Cadell, The Life and Works of a Scottish Colourist*, Edinburgh, 1988, p.89 (illus.)

Cadell's preoccupation with the effects of diffuse light on formally composed interiors continued throughout the 1920s and 30s and are a far cry from the more more vivacious Colourist essays of his early years. This example, painted around 1934, shows part of the studio in Regent Terrace. The soft blue light and domesticity of the scene belie the tension he has carefully contrived by repeatedly breaking flat planes, such as the painting and the easel.
By this time, with only three more years to live, Cadell was severely disillusioned by his lack of commercial success and was living in virtual poverty.

Plate 67

SAMUEL JOHN PEPLOE RSA (1871-1935) *Still Life with Japanese Jar and Roses* oil on canvas 18 x 16 inches signed (bottom left)

Exhibited: Aberdeen Art Gallery, 'Paintings from North-East Homes', 1951 (No.94),'Sir Thomas Jaffrey Exhibition', 1955 (No.81)

Probably painted circa 1919 when Peploe was self-confessedly endeavouring to paint the 'perfect' still-life. Peploe always remained the most 'colourist' of the Scottish Colourists and the bold palette he used in works such as this, painted onto a white ground, have an almost 'Jazz Age' resonance.

Plate 68

SIR WILLIAM MACTAGGART HRA PRSA (1903-1981) *The Castle in Snow* oil on canvas 30 x 36 inches signed (lower left)

Exhibited: Royal Scottish Academy, 1937 (No.465)

Painted with an unusually limited tonal range, this painting shows the extent of the influence of the contemporary French School on Mactaggart in the pre-war years. At this stage he still signed himself 'Jnr' to avoid confusion with his grandfather who had died in 1910

Other Works of Art

Plate 69

Sir John Steell (1804-1891)
Alexander and Bucephalus

Plate 70

Jessie Marion King (1875-1949)
The Ali Baba Vase

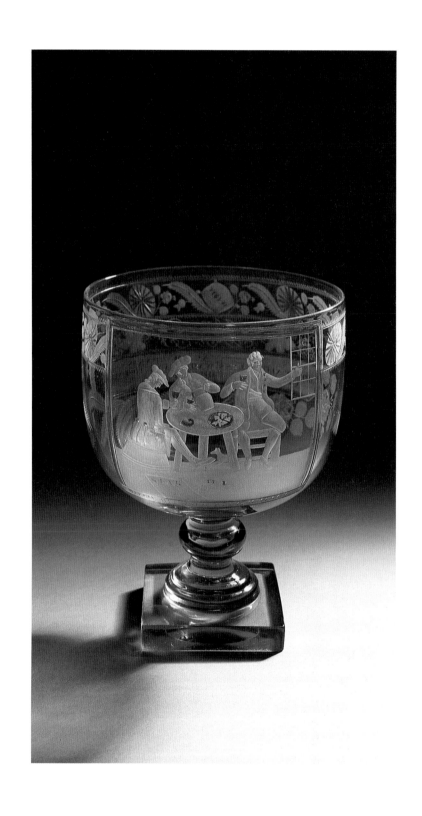

Plate 71

Circular Engraved Punch Bowl, possibly Scottish, 1824

Plate 72

*A Selection of Engraved and Enamelled
Dutch and English Wine Glasses*

Plate 73

John Linnell (1792-1882)
Storm in Harvest

90

Plate 74

Richard Ansdell (1815-1885)
The Deer Forest

Plate 75

Scottish Silver 'Bullet' Teapot 1729

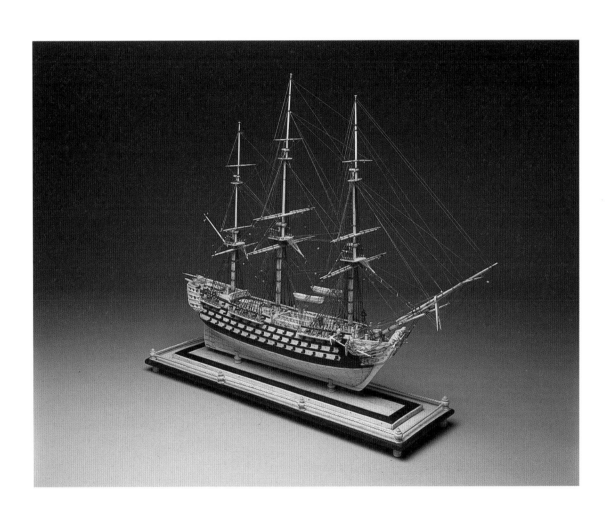

Plate 76

A Napoleonic Prisoner of War Ship Model, c. 1815

Plate 77

Louise Rayner (1832-1924)
The High Street from the West Bow, Edinburgh

- Other Works of Art -

Plate 69

SIR JOHN STEELL RSA (1804-1891) *Alexander Taming Bucephalus* bronze height: 19½ inches

Steell, who trained in Edinburgh and Rome, was one of the most celebrated Victorian sculptors and was appointed Sculptor in Ordinary to Her Majesty the Queen in 1838. The original of this statue was a massive piece carved in wood for the North British Fire and Insurance Corporation. A full size bronze was cast in 1832 and a number of smaller versions, like this example, the following year. The full scale bronze was purchased for the City of Edinburgh in 1884 and now stands outside the City Chambers.

Plate 70

JESSIE MARION KING (1875-1949) *The Ali Baba Vase* hand-painted pottery vase height: 15½ inches signed with monogram

Literature: Colin White, *The Enchanted World of Jessie M King*, Edinburgh, 1989, p.108, p.111(illus.)

Jessie King was part of the circle of artists and designers (notably Charles Rennie MacKintosh) who emerged from Glasgow School of Art in the 1890s. Primarily a book illustrator, she also worked in other mediums and during the 1920s and 30s turned to pottery. This is probably the finest example of her work from this period.

Plate 71

CIRCULAR PUNCH BOWL on heavy knopped stem and square base, with engraved tavern scene; reverse engraved with a dedication and date '1824'; possibly made in Edinburgh;
Height: 9⅝ inches Diameter (bowl): 7 inches

Plate 72

a) ENAMELLED WINE GLASS by the Beilby Family of Newcastle, c.1765; the bowl enamelled with a *lion sejeant* and the motto 'servir de bon vouloir le roy'.
Height: 7 ⅝ inches

The Beilby family were the foremost enamellers of glassware in the later half of the eighteenth century. They worked in Newcastle, enamelling glasses, tumblers, bowls and decanters with coats of arms, mottoes and classical and sporting scenes (see also glass *e*). The decoration of this glass would seem to be by two hands: possibly that of William Beilby for the delicate cartouche and Ralph or Mary (brother and sister), the crest and arms. The motto is that of Earl Grey of Northumberland

b) DUTCH ENGRAVED ROYAL ARMORIAL LIGHT BALUSTER GOBLET, engraved with the Royal Arms of Great Britain, the reverse with seven arrows tied in a ribbon, c.1760.
Height: 7½ inches

Intended to celebrate the twenty-fifth wedding anniversary of George II's daughter, Princess Anne, and Prince Willem IV of Orange who married in 1734. The seven arrows represent the seven provinces of the Netherlands.

c) DUTCH ENGRAVED LIGHT BALUSTER SHIPPING GOBLET, engraved with a three-masted ship and a coat of arms and motto
Height: 10 inches

The inscription reads 'success to the voyage of the *Boeken Roode*'. The *Boeken Roode* was built in Amsterdam in 1729 by the English Shipwright Thomas Davis as a ship of the line for the Dutch admiralty. It was traditional to give engraved goblets to wish success to the owner or captain of a new vessel. The clarity and accuracy of the engraving on this glass shows an armament of 44 guns, rather than the original 52 guns, suggesting that the glass was intended to commemorate her later re-commissioning under Captain Dirk Roos, whose family crest appears on the rear of the goblet. She saw action during the War of Austrian Succession and remained in active commission until the 1770s. The ship's log is preserved in the archives of the Dutch Admiralty College.

d) DUTCH STIPPLE ENGRAVED WINE GLASS, possibly by David Wolff, c.1770; 'Newcastle' composite stem; the bowl engraved with three *putti*.
Height: 5 inches

Dutch engravers perfected the art of stipple engraving on glass in the late 18th century. This glass is from an allegorical series depicting 'Liberty', 'Friendship, 'Harmony and 'Fatherland'.

e) ENAMELLED GOBLET by the Beilby Family, with the dedication 'Success to the Town and Trade of Leith', c.1765
Height: 7½ inches

Beilby decorated items with Scottish connections are extremely rare.

- Other Works of Art -

Plate 73

JOHN LINNELL (1792-1882) *Storm in Harvest* oil on canvas 37 x 53¼ inches signed and dated 1856 (lower left)

Exhibited: Royal Academy *Works by Old Masters and deceased Masters of the English School*, 1883
Literature: Alfred T Storey, *Life of John Linnell*, London, 1892, p.274

This is one of the few works of art in the Drambuie Collection that has no direct Scottish connection. However, it is an outstanding British painting of the 19th Century and is illustrated here without apology. The artist, John Linnell, entered the Royal Academy Schools at the age of thirteen under the patronage of John Varley and Benjamin West. However, he never quite fulfilled his early promise and is now better known for his friendship with and patronage of William Blake and, later, his son-in-law, Samuel Palmer.
Sharing with these two artists a distinct visionary streak, Linnell was concerned with the mystical grandeur of nature and in his finest paintings, painted in Surrey in the 1850s and 60s, conveys a vivid, rich and dramatic impression of humanity overcome by the God-given ferocity of nature.

Plate 74

RICHARD ANSDELL RA (1815-1885) *The Deer Forest* oil on canvas 65 x 30 inches signed and indistinctly dated (lower left), signed and inscribed with title on label (verso)

A Liverpool sporting and animal painter, Ansdell started painting in Scotland as early as the 1840s and, with his compatriot, Landseer, led the vogue for such subjects, which were exhibited at the Royal Academy to great success. One of the major animal painters of his generation, Ansdell made something of a speciality of unusually-sized pictures, both vertical and horizontal formats, which were often *tours de force* of ingenious composition.

Plate 75

A GEORGE II SILVER 'BULLET' TEAPOT by James Taitt, Edinburgh 1729 silver with wood fillets on handle Height: 6 inches

A very fine example of Scottish silver from the early 18th century. It is known that a jeweller and silversmith called 'Tate' accompanied Prince Charles Edward back to France in 1746 and it is tempting to think it might have been the maker of this teapot.

Plate 76

A NAPOLEONIC PRISONER OF WAR SHIP MODEL carved bone and horn 19 x 29 inches c.1815

French prisoners of war were held in Scotland and England during Napoleon's campaigns and many occupied their time making superb models which they would sell locally to get money for food and other necessities. Constructed out of what materials were at hand - bone, ivory, straw, horse hair and, even, human hair - the models reflected the experience and knowledge of the prisoners: religious objects, well-known building, ships and boats, sometimes working models of guillotines. This model of a fully-rigged 124- gun Man o'War is accurate in every detail and is remarkably well-preserved.

Plate 77

LOUISE RAYNER (1832-1924) *The High Street from the West Bow, Edinburgh* watercolour 22½ x 18¼ inches signed (lower left)

Along with Helen Allingham and Rose Barton, Louise Rayner was one of the most successful lady watercolourists of her generation. She specialised in English townscapes, particularly in the Cotswolds, only visiting Edinburgh quite late in her career. In this work her command of atmosphere and incidental detail is shown off to superb effect.